ARETHA'S FOOD for THE MIND

There Is a Way to A Better You!

By Aretha Tisdale

ISBN: 978-1-955312-38-7

Printed in the United States of America
Story Corner Publishing & Consulting, Inc.
1510 Atlanta Ave.
Portsmouth, VA 23704

Storycornerpublishing@yahoo.com
www.StoryCornerPublishing.com

Dedication

This book is dedicated in the loving memory of my parents, Eddie & Sadie McElroy. My parents taught me I could do anything if I put my mind to it.

My prayer is that I live the McElroy name to the fullest and do great exploits on the earth, in Jesus's name!

I also dedicate this book to my amazing husband, Calvin Tisdale Jr.

Calvin, thank you for being my number one supporter! You have always been my greatest motivator. Thank you for reminding me daily of the greatness inside of me, even when I cannot see. Your strong belief in me motivated me to move forward with this project and get it done.

Foreword

As a pastor, mentor, teacher, author, and former Healthcare Executive, I have had great pleasure observing and sharing in Aretha's relentless pursuit of her goals and vision. I have great confidence in her as an encourager, servant leader, relentless prayer intercessor, and woman of integrity. I have known Aretha for a couple of years, and I'm still in awe of her growth, determination, and perseverance to complete this phenomenal project.

Aretha has a passion for food and the relationship that it correlates with the mind, body, and spirit. I believe that God has given her this unique project and revelation of how to bridge the gap for the Kingdom with a pure heart to manifest transformation.

In this book, God uses Aretha Tisdale to cultivate an atmosphere that will allow the readers to fulfill their hunger in the natural and spiritual realm.

Matthew 5:6 KJV, "Blessed are they which do hunger and thirst after righteousness: for they shall be filled."

My prayer is that you will read this book with expectancy, hunger, and a thirst that will be filled by the natural and spiritual food, the Word of God.

Matthew 4:4 KJV, "But he answered and said, it is written, man shall not live by bread alone, but by every word that proceedeth out of the mouth of God."

I also pray that you will allow the gift of "Aretha the Encourager" to uplift, motivate, and nourish you with scriptures and recipes that will cause transformation in your mind, body, and spirit.

Dr. Patricia K, James DBS, RDN, CHC

Pastor of MyHeart2U Healing & Deliverance Community Church and Founder: PKJ Global Ministries & PCM Academy

Table of Contents

Acknowledgments

I first want to acknowledge God because, without Him, I would not have written this book.

I want to thank Dr. Patricia K. James for encouraging me to get this project completed and not allow greatness to lie dormant on the inside of me. Dr. James, I am grateful that you believed I had what it took and that God equipped me to write this book.

Also, I would like to thank all my family who inspired me to continue writing until this project was complete.

I give a special thank you to our wonderful children: Calvin Tisdale III, Latasha McElroy, Jarvis Johnson, Darren McElroy, Ebony McElroy, and Sherrica Edwards.

I even want to thank our new son and daughters: Jaquay Edwards, Lauren Johnson, Kee'Ana McElroy, Jcoby Mixon, and Zaiden Rone.

I even acknowledge our 20 grandchildren for their encouragement: Samiah Tisdale, Ariel Tisdale, Chloe Tisdale, Emmeri Tisdale, Jordan McElroy, Jayden McElroy, Journey McElroy, Jo'ziah McElroy, Jayvion Johnson, Janiah Johnson, Annalise Johnson, Kariah McElroy, Kobe McElroy, Kyson McElroy, Kylo McElroy, Kenzo McElroy, Kaydence Mixon, Kayden Mixon, Ryleigh Edwards, and Rylan Edwards.

You all are my rock! You all helped shape and mold me into the woman I am today. So, for that, I say thank you!

I also thank all my friends who believed in me and have supported my vision. Thank you all for helping me as I got into position to obey God's assignment for my life. I want to especially thank Jill Hudson, who has always seen more in me than I could have ever seen in myself. Thank you for your inspiration.

Last but not least, I want to acknowledge the loving memory of my granddaughter Grace Faith McElroy and daughter-in-law Equisha Tisdale for the joy they brought to my life.

Introduction

Since college, I've known that I would one day write a book after my professor expressed her desire to read more of my writings. She told me I needed to write a book after reading an assignment I submitted to her. My professor stated how she was speechless as I sat in her office. She expressed that I captured her attention from the beginning and kept it throughout the entire assignment. My professor also stated she was hungry for more, and I needed to write a part two to my project. I was in amazement and could not believe what I was hearing. She looked at me and said, "You will write a book one day." Well, that one day has finally come!

Low and behold, I became connected with Dr. Patricia K. James. After many years of not hearing anything else about writing a book, Dr. Patricia told me I needed to write a cookbook. In no way are these two ladies connected. It was two different states and about a ten-year gap in between. I was taken back to my professor's office when Dr. Patricia said the very same thing as my professor. At that moment, I knew God intended for me to write this book. It came to a point where God prompted and guided me to write by telling me what I was to say in the book. I kept going back and forward with thoughts in my mind. I did not think I could accomplish the assignment of this book.

God had allowed others to see what He had placed on the inside of me before I realized the talents, abilities, and gifts that were lying dormant on the inside of me. I submitted to God and gave Him a "Yes" to writing this book along with others. Since then, God has been encouraging me along the way. God began to tell me He built me for this. He referred to me as the righteousness of God and that I could persevere until the end. All I could say was, "here I am, Lord. Use me."

God gave me the directions of writing about food for the mind, body, and spirit to allow readers to get fed through my life experiences. There is also nourishment from scriptures, recipes, and the power to lead and live a faith-filled life through God. I pray these pages will resonate with each of you and cause the transformation in your life. *Romans*

12:2 NIV, *"And be not conform to this world: but be ye transformed by the renewing of your mind, that ye may prove what is that good, and acceptable, and perfect will of God."*

Every time I would tell God all that was wrong in my life and why I could not write this book, He began to push me. God would say, "you can do this, get focused, rid yourself of distractions, and get busy." The Lord started telling me all the reasons I was the right fit to get this book written. He had me look back over my life's experiences and reminded me that they could help others get through their current situations and circumstances. *Romans 8:28 NIV, "And we know that in all things God works for the good of those who love him, who have been called according to his purpose." Amen.*

I realized God has me in transition for my position to get bigger and better. He is pushing me into my place of purpose in life. I must move ahead into destiny and out of history because that has already passed. *Philippians 3:13 KJV, "I count not myself to have apprehended: but this one thing I do, forgetting those things which are behind and reaching forth unto those things which are before, I press toward the mark for the prize of the high calling of God in Christ Jesus."* My future was often unclear, but I'm confident now of who knows.

So, I believe *Jeremiah 29:11 KJV, "For I know the thoughts that I think towards you, saith the Lord, thoughts of peace and not of evil, to give you an expected end."*

God had written the story of my life before I was in my mother's womb. I know now without a shadow of a doubt God has a purpose for me. Blessings to each of you who will read this book. I pray you will be inspired in Jesus's name!

Prayer of Serenity

God grant me the serenity to accept the things I cannot change;

Courage to change the things I can;

And wisdom to know the difference. Living one day at a time;

Enjoying one moment at a time;

Accepting hardships as the pathway to peace;

Taking, as He did, this sinful world as it is, not as I would have it;

Trusting that He will make all things right If I surrender to His will;

So that I may be reasonably happy in this life and supremely happy with Him Forever and ever in the next.

Amen!

CHAPTER 1
The Mind

The mind is the faculty of consciousness and thought that enables a person to be aware of the world and their experiences to think or feel. It controls the intellect, reason, and thoughts. The heart and mind are both needed for Biblical faith according *to Ephesians 2: 8-10 KJV*, *"For by grace are ye saved through faith; and that not of yourselves: it is the gift of God: Not of works, lest any man should boast. For we are his workmanship, created in Christ Jesus unto good works, which God hath before ordained that we should walk in them."* So, we must do as *Philippians 2:5 NIV, "Let this mind be in you, which was in Christ Jesus."*

When it comes to mind control, I can remember how I allowed someone to control, manipulate, abuse, and intimidate me. I was in an unhealthy relationship for eight years, just for it to abruptly end and find out I was not even in love. I remember how I allowed my mind to play tricks on me by having me think I needed to stay for the sake of my children. I would get over the hurt and pain he had caused physically, mentally, emotionally, and verbally by focusing on my children. I knew change had to happen once the abuse became worse. It was so bad that I would be beaten and choked as I gasped for air on the verge of passing out. I would barely be able to breathe, move, or say anything. All I could do was cry and pray that my children were not traumatized. Everything was his way or no way at all! He always wanted to be in control until it was time to provide financially or father our children. I would call the police, but fear would set in, and I would not press charges on him. The police would advise me to write a report about the incidents, but I was just relieved they showed up.

My dad asked me if I would stay until he killed me? I do not remember if I even answered that question before my dad continued. He said stalking and physical abuse leads to serious harm, even death in most cases. My dad told me to get out of the relationship out of concern. I eventually did leave that relationship, but not exactly when my dad advised me. It was not until I had suffered more physical, verbal, mental, and emotional abuse. I went through shame, disappointment, and guilt. I soon realized the relationship was going nowhere.

My dad and I were traveling down Interstate 65 in Mobile, Alabama, one day. He told me to read a billboard we were passing. It read: He beat her ninety-nine times, but he only gave her flowers once. There was also a picture of a casket with flowers on the top. I knew that had to be a revelation for me. That was the moment I knew it was not healthy for me to continue in that relationship exposing my children to all the chaos and confusion that was going on. I was teaching my daughters the opposite of what love was. I showed them love was accepting abuse. I also taught my son that it was okay to abuse women because I stayed so long and even made excuses.

I knew there had to be more to life than a toxic relationship. I wanted better for myself and my children. Love will never beat on you. Love will never disrespect you or your loved ones. Love will never do you wrong. Love will never make you stay out all night. Love will not make one show off in the presence of others. I could go on and on. I knew I was not in love after opening my eyes to the truth. I guess I did not want to be alone at some point. It was time to exit that relationship quickly, or I would have been in trouble. When I tried letting him know the relationship was over, he began to do more stalking. He even stalked the guys I would date and confronted them to cause a confrontation.

I grew so tired of him causing chaos in my life that I cut all communication with him and prayed he would move on. That did not work out too well because he showed up at my house and started a physical fight with me. That was the day I defended myself, which shocked him. At that point, I was not taking any more physical abuse, period. I was done with him and did not give him any more access to control me. It was time to sever the ties, so I did. I was no longer going to expose my children to that type of behavior.

My mother would tell me how he would pass by her house with a woman in the car every morning because he knew she would be standing outside. He wanted to see if he could get a rise out of me when that information came to me. My mother said she wanted to tell me for a long time, but she knew I would not receive it because I was so-called in love. My mother would always tell me that I was too good for what I allowed to go on in my life. She said this should not be happening.

My mother knew I was serious about being over him and ready to move on once I told her. She began to say to me that God has someone in store for me, so be patient. I then called my aunt and told her what I was going through, and she said God was going to send the right man to my doorstep. She was unsure if she would live to see it happen, but she was confident that I would know it when I saw him. God did exactly that! The right man did show up on my doorstep with ferns, and I did not know how to take care of them. I did try, though. Taking care of the ferns was therapeutic for me. It helped me take my mind off the abuse I had gone through.

At first, I thought the relationship was not going to work because of our age difference, but he turned out to be the best man that has happened to me! I almost lost my GOOD THING with stinking thinking. We have been married for twenty-one years, and I thank God for a man of his caliber.

God was granting me grace back when I did not know anything about it. It only took me five weeks to get my ex-boyfriend entirely out of my system. I thought it would take forever to get myself together because of all I poured into that relationship over so many years. Once I was done, I did not even look back! It was only God who got me through so quickly. Let me encourage you. God does hear and answer prayers, so continue to pray. Even if you do not know how to pray or can only recite *The Lord's prayer*, remember prayer is just a conversation with God. Prayer is sufficient and essential for every situation!

-Always Stop and Pray!

I was in a place of brokenness, and I know now God had a plan for my life! What an awesome God we serve! There was much negative talk about the man God sent me to forfeit my blessing. People were telling me he was married, but he wasn't. He had recently gotten out of a relationship. You would have thought people wanted to see me happy after all I went through in my past, but they didn't. They wanted to continue to see me broken and alone. I'm glad I did not listen to the people.

I thank God for blessing me with a man that loves Him and believes in doing as the Bible commands. He strives to live a life pleasing to our Father. God, all along, had an excellent plan for my life. I thought my plans were the way to go, but clearly, they were not.

Jeremiah 29:11 NIV, "For I know the plans I have for you, declares the Lord, plans to prosper you, and not to harm you, plans to give you hope and a future."

LOOK AT GOD! I am in awe of Him.

I remember my abuser telling me no one would want to be with me because he would tell lies on me. He thought everyone would believe what he had to say and turn away from me. Some did believe and turned away. Many stopped speaking to me and even stopped being cordial with me until they later found out the truth. I realized that all those who dropped off because of the lies never needed to be connected to me in the first place. When they turned away or stopped talking to me, it was a win for me. They moved out the way for new people to enter my life. God allowed the right man to find me. He did not believe the lies that floated around about me because he knew what God showed him. He believed in God and knew I was the woman for him. Glory!!!!

Job 22:28 KJV, "Thou shalt also decree a thing, and it shall be established unto thee: and the light shall shine upon thy ways."

I did not allow my heart to wax cold towards my abuser; instead, I prayed for him to be saved by God. I prayed for him to desire to have a relationship with Jesus Christ. I knew it was only a matter of time before he accepted Jesus as his personal Lord and Savior.

A word of advice, leave any relationship that does not value or appreciate you! You are enough and matter in the eyes of God! You are worth so much more than you think! Jesus died for us because we mean that much to Him. I thank God for the test I went through to have a testimony to share with you all. My heart is to help someone struggling with physical and mental abuse.

Get up! Get moving towards the life God has designed for you! That mess was my message, and the test was my testimony.

Father God,

I pray that anyone who reads this book in an abusive relationship is freed today in Jesus's name. I pray they will not have to hurt or suffer any longer in that unhealthy relationship. I pray that you will open the doors of freedom and healing to them, and they will receive, in Jesus's mighty name, Amen.

Did I ever tell you about the time?

-When I almost died from a medical illness I did not know I had.

-When I was a single mother struggling to make ends meet, only having assistance from my parents and the government.

-When I was so sick, and all I could do was look up towards Heaven, not able to mutter a word because I was in so much pain.

-When I lost everything, the Lord called my family and me to relocate to another state. The Lord then restored us.

-When many turned their back on me when I said "Yes" to God.

-When I only had good intentions for many, they took my kindness for weakness.

-When my husband became ill after moving to a new town with no family or friends close.

-When many close to me wouldn't support me with the vision God had given me.

-When I didn't have a dime and nowhere to get one from either. All I could do was pray and wait on God.

-When I did not have transportation, and I needed a ride.

-When I almost got evicted, but the Lord saw us through.

-When no matter how faithful and loyal I was to others, it was not reciprocated back to me.

-When I gave from my heart and a place of sacrifice but did not even receive a thank you in return.

-When I brought sincerity, authenticity, trustworthiness, and integrity to the table, but I did not receive it in return.

-When my sciatica nerve was so bad, I had to drag my legs to do my workout routine. I persevered.

-When everything that could go wrong did, and the Lord reminded me to show up still.

-When all my bills were due, there was a decrease in our income.

-When I needed surgery, my job immediately terminated me for being out for an excessive amount of time.

-When I did for others, and in my doing for them, they were talking behind my back.

-When I wanted to give up, but God said to me, "Hang in there. The best is yet to come!"

-When there were times my husband would do projects for customers, they would refuse to pay for the orders.

-When I tried to reach out, many did not reach back.

-When I had to pray but could not get a word out.

-When God led me to do live videos, I was scared. I knew I had to do it afraid.

-When I couldn't stay focused on the critical things that mattered in my life because so much was pressing upon me. I allowed myself to become distracted.

I'll stop here, but there is so much more that I went through. I thank God for changing my situation!

Guard your mind!

Keep watch over who and what you are allowing into your life. Remember, the devil only comes to steal, kill, and destroy. God wants you to have an abundant life of blessings. Do not fall victim to Satan's tactics. He does not love you.

If you let the enemy control your thoughts, he will direct your whole life, which will lead you to a place you do not want to be. Leave him out!!!!!

Three ways to guard your mind:

1. Recognize ungodly thoughts and ideas by testing them against God's Word. Everything that glitters is not gold! Check all actions and motives of others against the Word of God!!!!! Run if they do not line up!!!

2. You must reject the ungodly according to God's Word. Stay woke in this hour! *1 Peter 5:8 NIV, "Be sober, and vigilant: because your adversary the devil, as a roaring lion, walketh about, seeking whom he may devour."* Be watchful and mindful of your surroundings, your circle, your groups, your friends, and your family because the enemy could be lurking anywhere.

3. You may at times need to command the devil to leave in Jesus's name! *James 4:7-8 NIV, "Submit yourselves therefore to God. Resist the devil, and he will flee from you. Draw nigh to God, and he will draw nigh unto you. Cleanse your hands, ye sinners: and purify your hearts, ye double minded."* Do not allow Satan to take residence in your head. Serve him notice of eviction today and let him know he must go! He has overstayed his welcome. Decide to make a change for the better because God will see you through whatever situation you face. No longer should you allow him to make your mind his playground and workshop. Tell him to have recess someplace else because you are seated at the right hand of Christ. You shall not be moved. The seat is a location, and a position of authority believers possess in Jesus Christ!

Amen!

JOURNAL YOUR EXPERIENCE

Philippians 4:7 NIV,
"And the peace of God, which transcends all understanding,
will guard your hearts and your minds in Christ Jesus."

Romans 12:2 NIV,
"Do not conform to the pattern of this world, but be transformed
by the renewing of your mind. Then you will be able to test and
approve what God's will is—his good, pleasing and perfect will."

Isaiah 26:3 NIV,
"You will keep in perfect peace those whose minds a
steadfast, because they trust in you."

2 Timothy 1:7 NIV,
"For the Spirit God gave us does not make us timid,
but gives us power, love and self-discipline."

Note:

CHAPTER 2
Mind Control

Mind control is also known as manipulation, thought reform, brainwashing, mental control, malignant use of group dynamics, and many other names.

Also, these are signs of witchcraft (control). If you encounter this, pray that these demonic spirits are broken and destroyed. Command and cast them to the dry places away from you and your family, in Jesus's name!

Matthew 21:21-22 KJV, "Jesus answered and said unto them, verily I say unto you, if ye have faith, and doubt not, ye shall not only do this which is done to the fig tree, but also if ye shall say unto this mountain! Be thou removed, and be thou cast into the sea, it shall be done. And all things whatsoever ye shall ask in prayer, believing ye shall receive."

Acts 10:34 NIV, "Then Peter opened his mouth, and said, of a truth I perceive that God is no respecter of persons:"

Psalm 30:5-6 KJV, "For his anger endureth but a moment; in his favour is life, weeping may endure for a night, but joy cometh in the morning. And in my prosperity, I said, I shall never be moved."

Here are a few ways to know if someone is using mind control against you:

1. Isolation- If you find that you are beginning to become isolated from family, friends, etc. That could be a sign that someone is trying to get you alone to take advantage of you. Avoid disconnecting from people you need in your life.

2. Moody behavior- Ask yourself, do I change behavior to prevent or stop an argument? That could open the door to mind control if your emotions are swayed by what another does or behaves. You can also be classified as a follower. I began to learn and develop leadership skills. Please do not fall victim to becoming a follower because predators can sense it and, in turn, take advantage. Lead with excellence, and do not be afraid!

3. Metacommunication- Nonverbal cues: Allowing someone to control how you respond to a situation is a good example. God has given you your mind to think clearly and accurately, so use

it!

4. Neuro-Linguistic Programming (NLP) is a pseudoscientific approach to communication, personal development, and psychotherapy. NLP is a connection between neurological processes (neuro-), language (linguistic), and behavioral patterns learned through experience (programming). NLP can treat phobias, depression, tic disorders, psychosomatic illnesses, near-sightedness, allergy, the common cold, and learning disorders. When NLP is used to deceive someone, they evaluate many aspects and use language to plant suggestions. NLP coaches you in to what the person desires you to do. Beware of slicksters, fast talkers, and con artists. They only want to get personal gain from your possession. Be careful and stay watchful!

5. Uncompromising Rules- Someone may place unreasonable rules on your lifestyle. If unrealistic deadlines, strictly regulated mealtimes, monitored bathroom breaks, or decreased personal time is your portion, consider mind control at work. Or even if you are cut off from your own money or friends, this could be another red flag. Be vigilant and sober in this hour!

I remember how Satan would try to take control of my mind until I let him know that I am a child of the Most High God and He loves me. I stood against Satan, cluttering my mind and heart with stinking thinking.

James 1:8 KJV, "A double-minded man is unstable in all his ways."

JOURNAL YOUR EXPERIENCE

Philippians 4:7 NIV,
"And the peace of God, which transcends all understandin
will guard your hearts and your minds in Christ Jesus."

Romans 12:2 NIV,
"Do not conform to the pattern of this world, but be transformed
by the renewing of your mind. Then you will be able to test and
approve what God's will is—his good, pleasing and perfect will."

Isaiah 26:3 NIV,
"You will keep in perfect peace those whose minds a
steadfast, because they trust in you."

2 Timothy 1:7 NIV,
"For the Spirit God gave us does not make us timid
but gives us power, love and self-discipline."

Note:

CHAPTER 3
Power of The Mind

Imagination (mind) creates something in the spiritual realm manifested in the physical realm. "The Power of the Mind" is the same strategy Jesus Christ followed.

The Power of the mind focuses on your thoughts. What you think, you can become! What do you think about yourself? The ideas you choose to entertain influence your actions. The things you find yourself doing all start with a thought in your mind. Your beliefs, mindset, and attitude influence how you behave or respond to specific events. Only the Bible can unveil the misery of the mind and its power. The Word of God is what shifts us for good.

God's Word reminds us, according to *Hebrews 12:2 KJV*, *"looking unto Jesus the author and finisher of our faith; who for the joy that was set before him endured the cross, despising the shame, and is set down at the right hand of the throne of God."*

The mind is very powerful. The thoughts we think give our bodies and minds energy to complete a task. Our mind controls actions such as moving our arms up and down. So, the energy we put into action is the energy we must put into words. If you think you can do it, then it can be done!

Philippians 4:13 KJV, "I can do all things through Christ that strengthens me."

The key to health and happiness is a peaceful and positive mind. Free yourself from anything that does not bring peace in your life the way God intended for you to have. The peace of God surpasses all understanding.

1 Corinthians 14:33 KJV, "For God is not the author of confusion, but of peace, as in all churches of the saints."

The Locked Door

I had a dream one night that people I knew very well were having an event. Therefore, I agreed to attend the event. As I pulled up and went inside, many familiar people were there. So, I thought. I began to get comfortable and felt I had made the right decision to attend. I told a few of the ladies that I must go to my car because I had left my phone there. The house was on a dirt road in a rural area, and it was very dark. I then asked who would walk with me out to my car. Two of the women there agreed. As we were approaching my car, numerous people walked down the road. The two women with me said we must go back inside because we did not know those people. Therefore, we began to run back to the door to get into the house. They locked the door on me as I reached for the handle, leaving me outside. I tried to keep up with them, but I fell behind, which gave them a head-start into the house.

They were standing on the other side of the door, looking out the window directly at me. I pleaded with the women to let me inside, but they just looked at me as if they did not recognize me. The people walking down the road had finally made it to the house. I was afraid because I had no idea of their intent. I turned around to look at the people in their faces. That's when I realized they did not come to harm me. Something in my spirit instantly connected me to those people, and I was at peace. One of the gentlemen then said they were there to rescue me because I was in danger. I asked, "how?" They revealed that the women who accompanied me made plans for a group of people to harm me. Then the women would act as if they did not know what happened or who the people were. The people walking down the road were the only reason the evil men did not carry out the plan the women hired them to do.

I was in disbelief. I told the people standing before me that I knew the women very well and they would not do as such. They told me I did not know the women at all but only knew the version of them that they wanted me to believe. The man said our Heavenly Father sent them to rescue me because the women had a dangerous plot against me. He then reiterated that I did not know the women as well as I thought.

The man assured me that the group of people did not come to harm me. They wanted to get me to safety. I was devastated to know these people were telling the truth about the two women who walked me to my car. I was always kind to them, so I did not understand why they wanted to harm me. The man said it was just a trick of the enemy. Satan used them to act in such a way it scared me.

John 10:10 KJV, "The thief cometh not, but to steal, and to kill, and to destroy: I am come that they might have life and have it more abundantly."

It turns out I did not know the women as well as I thought. The man said if they had not been walking down the road for me, the evil men the women hired would have hurt me very badly. The man from the rescue group said the hired men were going to vandalize my car, harass me, hold me hostage, and do anything they could to torment me. The reason was that I am who God says I am. I remember saying, "OH MY GOD!" I woke up from that dream thinking, "God, you saved me yet again!" I thought, "lookout, Satan! I am the apple of God's eye." Even though that dream was many years ago, I'm still very cautious of where I go, who I commune with, and entertain. My mother used to say, "everyone that smiles in your face is not your friend. People will stab you in the back when you are not looking. Therefore, be careful who occupies your space!" I will add to that by saying, "no matter how good you pretend to be, the real personality will appear."

Be careful in this hour not to fellowship with Satan! No good will come from being in fellowship with him! One more time, Satan only comes to steal, kill, and destroy! Don't be his next victim!

Romans 12:1-2 KJV, "I beseech you therefore, brethren, by the mercies of God, that ye present your bodies a living sacrifice, holy, acceptable unto God, which is your reasonable service. And be not conformed to this world: but be ye transformed by the renewing of your mind, that ye may prove what is that good, and acceptable, and perfect, will of God."

Isaiah 26:3 KJV, "Thou wilt keep him in perfect peace, whose mind is stayed on thee: because he trusteth in thee."

Our mind projects an image to us so we can complete the action. All of this happens from a thought that enters our brain. Be careful of the thoughts you think because if they are idled long enough, they become a reality and are put into action. Don't let Satan deceive you.

Visualize good thoughts. Ask God for the desires of your heart and leave them in His hands. Believe in faith that He will do it, so there is no room for the enemy to get in. Faith will unlock every situation in your life.

Hebrews 11:1 KJV, "Now faith is the substance of things hoped for, the evidence of things not seen."

You must speak into existence what you want to see happen in your life. Say it until you see what you spoke. Open your mouth and speak it into the atmosphere.

Hebrews 11:6 KJV, "But without faith it is impossible to please him: for he that cometh to God must believe that he is, and that he is a rewarder of them that diligently seek him."

Our words have power! Always speak the right words in the right season to the right people!

Romans 10:17 KJV, "So then faith cometh by hearing and hearing by the word of God."

Stay in the Word and allow the Word to come alive inside of you! Remember, Jesus created every miracle in His mind before He physically did it. See, Jesus did not pray alone. He engaged the Power of the Mind to understand what God was showing Him concerning each day. We must do the same by clearing our minds to allow the Holy Spirit to flow. Set a place in your home conducive to the Holy Spirit to meet with you daily. I did! It is the best thing I could have ever done.

Make sure that you get the atmosphere set daily to keep your mind and heart focused on God. A time with God is an incredible experience! Make sure you are having a monologue and dialogue conversation. Speak and then listen for instructions. I realized I would always fail at hearing from God because I would do all the talking and leave after venting. I now know that was not how this was supposed to go. Allow the Holy Spirit guidance to lead you so that you will alleviate unnecessary heartache and headache down the road.

Going from Mad to Motivated

As I was preparing for work, I received a phone call that left me feeling frustrated and furious. After getting off the phone, I cried out to the Lord, asking Him to help me release the anger. I did not want to carry those feelings with me to work. The Lord began to bring familiar scriptures to my mind. As I recited them out of my mouth, I started feeling better. I continued getting ready for work, and the Lord gave me the assignment to motivate His people each morning once I got to work. I was confused and unsure of how to accomplish the mission, so I asked God for directions. The Lord told me what to do, and I quickly obeyed. Once I arrived to work, I spoke to my supervisor about doing motivational pep talks in the mornings with the staff, and she eagerly agreed. She was excited and in need of motivation for herself. Therefore, she asked if I could start immediately. I showed up ready the following day and never looked back! Now, I could have let what appeared to be a challenging phone call distract me from hearing God, but I didn't. Instead of running away from God in trying times, I ran to Him. I had no idea He would have had an assignment for me. It was so rewarding to know that God could heal me to help others all in the same day. I was honored that He would choose me to speak to His people at my job.

My co-workers enjoyed the motivational segments in the morning. They benefited from them so much that they did not want anyone else to do them. I realized at that moment that it was only the anointing of God that reached the people. It does not matter which vessel delivers the message, but God has to be the head of it all. If God does the anointing and appointing, the people will receive all they need. I was one hundred percent sure that God anointed and appointed me to fulfill the task. Therefore, no one else could take my place. I learned we all must stay in our lane when it comes to assignments. In the natural, it appears we are drunk driving if we are swerving from our lane to another's repeatedly. Therefore, why should we do that when it comes to spiritual assignments? No one can fulfill your position as you do. God created you for your assignments, and it is all part of your purpose in life.

DO WHAT YOU ARE CALLED TO DO IN YOUR LANE! In this season, do not try to fill someone else shoes. God has given each of us a pair that fits us perfectly.

God used a phone call to allow the Holy Spirit to minister to me before I was off to work. He allowed me to help others to have a more productive day. Who would have ever thought God would assign me to deliver motivational messages to my teammates? What an awesome

God we serve! We never know what others are dealing with before they leave their home.

Galatians 6:2 KJV, "Bear ye one another's burdens, and so fulfill the law of Christ."

You must lend a helping hand in this hour! A helping hand is not just considered monetary value. No one does anything alone. You can help friends, family, and coworkers to get through life's obstacles. Hopefully, they will do the same for you. God is always pleased when we share. You must consistently demonstrate love for the Lord and others by being compassionate and caring towards those you encounter. Even small gestures can mean a great deal.

That day of the phone call could've been much worse if I had not allowed the Holy Spirit to minister deep down in my soul that morning. After the Lord was finished with me, I forgot why I was so upset. God indeed is a mind fixer and heart regulator!

Double Suicide Contemplation

After getting out of a relationship and getting myself back on track, derogatory and degrading things were being said about me by my ex. I never heard any great things about me from my ex, only lies to get others to walk away. Many believed the stories about me. I was so hurt and discouraged. I was ready to give up! If I had known back then what I know now, I would be better off. I would not have endured so much heartache. Back then, I tried to defend myself and fight my own battles.

Exodus 14:14 KJV, "The Lord will fight for you, you have only to be still."

This scripture tells me I do not have to worry because God got me! I used to care what others thought of me. Since it was always negative, I thought suicide was my only way out. I wanted peace. I wanted to be loved and accepted.

One day I went into the room where my mother was sitting, and I told her I wanted to kill myself. I expressed my plan to overdose on pills to be done with life once and for all. I had the pills all laid out on my pillow, waiting for me. My mother was alarmed and sprang into action. She was able to talk me out of following through with my plan that day. I thank God for my mother because she was loving and caring. She knew just what to say to make me think positively about life. My mother always wanted the best for her children, especially me, because I went through so many trials.

I used to be ashamed to go out in public because I felt that the people were always staring at me. My mind would tell me they heard the lies about me and believed them, even if they were strangers. I also thought I would be alone forever because I listened to the people thinking my children were baggage. I figured since I was a mother of three and one on the way, no one would want to be with me. The thoughts of suicide would not let me rest. I had to keep pushing it to the back of my mind.

My oldest brother encouraged me when I could not speak over myself. He reminded me that God would fight my battles. He convinced me to focus on myself more and to find a church home where I could hear the Word of God daily. He even told me to begin reciting The Lord's Prayer every day to get it down into my spirit. I followed his instructions, and after a while, things got better. It was easier for me to let go of the past. I was over my ex, and it felt good. God helped me through the process. I was no longer bound to suicide, shame, disappointment, discouragement, or mediocrity either! I was FREE!

I did not know how to pray while going through darkness, but The Lord's Prayer started me on my journey. That was the same prayer Jesus taught the disciples to pray after they asked Him to teach them to pray. Prayer is just a heart-to-heart conversation with God our Father because He speaks back to us. After I allowed God in and became more comfortable with praying to Him, I took a course that helped me to pray even deeper. Prayer is what shifted my situation. Therefore, prayer is an essential key to all our lives. Now I am a Certified Global Prayer Intercessor and a Certified Global Servant Leader. I enjoy having conversations with God and will never go back to silence. I am now walking in God's purpose for my life, and it feels good. God created me to be an intercessor to pray on others' behalf that cannot pray for themselves. I thank God for trusting me with this particular task because I remember when I could not pray for myself. He assigned intercessors to pray for me until I had the confidence to pray for myself. A prayer as simple as The Lord's Prayer healed me from all the hurt and pain I had gone through. I did not understand how urgent it was for me to develop a prayer life until God revealed to me that the spirit of suicide wanted to also attach to my unborn baby.

Once my daughter got older, I discovered that the spirit of suicide was knocking on the door of her heart. She was a star basketball player in the 7th and 8th grade. Once she transitioned to high school, it all changed. Since she was a newcomer, they were extra hard on her, and she even experienced jealousy. One day my daughter told me she did not want to play basketball anymore. Therefore, I knew something was wrong because she loved to play. I decided to meet with the principal and coach concerning the matter and realized why my daughter did not want to play anymore. The school had an unfair process set in place. The newcomers were to sit on the bench until the coach felt the need to use them, which was never! I decided to transfer my daughter to another school, hoping the new basketball team would be fair and allow her to play. To our surprise, the situation was worse! She was invisible to them and not even allowed to touch a basketball.

My daughter is very talented at basketball, and I am not just saying that because I am her mother. They did not even give her a chance to show them what she had to offer the team. Most people don't believe some are gifted to play the sport. They think it's about how long you have practiced or played the game. My daughter grew so discouraged that she spoke to me about killing herself. She was tired of being mistreated and unheard. She was being treated poorly by the teammates and coaches. I felt so bad because I remembered wanting to kill myself while pregnant with her, unknowingly creating a cycle that needed to be broken. I knew I could not live with myself if she followed through with it. I also knew basketball was her passion because she came alive when she played. I asked her what other school she thought would be best to try. I was willing to help in any way I could. She told me Blount High School in Alabama was a school she wanted to give a try. We planned for her to travel there, and I am glad we did because the coach was fantastic! Hats off to him because he was indeed God sent!

He made her feel at home, and her teammates were happy to have her as part of their team. The coach was very informative and professional. He even helped her stay on track with her grades. After starting at the new high school, my daughter became happy again.

I know life will have more rollercoaster rides for her, but I pray that she overcomes the spirit of suicide when things get rough. I pray she would look to God for all her help and know that He will work everything out for her good as long as she continues to love Him.

Although, I often think about what could have happened if my daughter did not tell us her plan to commit suicide. As God's people, we should never accept abuse which leaves us thinking that suicide is the way out because God fights our battles if we allow Him. I am so thankful there is a God in Heaven who hears our prayers!

Father, God, in the name of Jesus,

I plead the blood of Jesus over the people of God and against the spirit of suicide. I bind the spirit of suicide off the people of God, and I command it to flee to the dry places in the name of Jesus. God, I pray that you protect your people from being tormented by this spirit any longer in Jesus's mighty name, Amen.

JOURNAL YOUR EXPERIENCE

Philippians 4:7 NIV,
"And the peace of God, which transcends all understandin
will guard your hearts and your minds in Christ Jesus."

Romans 12:2 NIV,
"Do not conform to the pattern of this world, but be transformed
by the renewing of your mind. Then you will be able to test and
approve what God's will is—his good, pleasing and perfect will."

Isaiah 26:3 NIV,
"You will keep in perfect peace those whose minds are
steadfast, because they trust in you."

2 Timothy 1:7 NIV,
"For the Spirit God gave us does not make us timid,
but gives us power, love and self-discipline."

Note:

CHAPTER 4
Mind of The Spirit

The mind of the spirit refers to everything controlled by the spirit. Your thoughts have power! When our mind is in line with the word of God, He will protect our spirit, soul, and body!

Know this: Every good idea is not a God idea!

Toxic thoughts such as stress, worry, fear, anger, and unforgiveness cause damage to the brain. Toxic thoughts even cause physical illness, lack of sleep and memory, etc.

2 Timothy 1:7 NIV, "For the Spirit God gave us does not make us timid, but gives us power, love and self-discipline."

When you guard your mind and keep yourself in an attitude of faith, praise, Thanksgiving, and truth, you will experience healing, deliverance, and victory.

Colossians 3:2 NIV, "Set your minds on things above, not on earthly things."

There are many spirits, so allow the Holy Spirit to take over your mind. Once we submit, we would be able to hear God clearly, experience joy, and encounter peace.

Isaiah 26:3-4 NIV, "You will keep in perfect peace those whose minds are steadfast, because they trust in you. Trust in the Lord forever, for the Lord, the Lord himself, is the Rock eternal."

We must keep our minds focused and fixated on the things of God. Allow the spirit of God to enter your mind and guide your life. Prayer will help you to tap into the Spirit.

Ephesians 4:23-24 KJV, "and be renewed in the spirit of your mind; and that ye put on the new man, which after God is created in righteousness and true holiness."

Romans 15:6 KJV, "that ye may with one mind and one mouth glorify God, even the Father of our Lord Jesus Christ."

From 4-2.5 To 6-3

The Lord blessed our family with a four-bedroom, 2.5 bath, two-story home. We loved that home, and it was an excellent fit for our family. I remember the realtor being very informational and informative.

She stayed connected with us for a while, even after signing the papers for our new lease to own home. We enjoyed every minute of our new home. The stairs were our favorite part! The children were so excited that they would clean their rooms daily and keep everything nice and neat. I really enjoyed cooking and baking in our large kitchen. Our home was cozy and comfortable.

After about six months of enjoying our home, the realtor called and asked me to view another home. She said it was bigger and better! I agreed and went that same day. When I pulled up to the house, I was blown away. As I walked through the house, I knew I just had to have it. I asked the realtor what I had to do to transition into this house, and she made it sound so easy. She assured me that since it was the same company handling the sale, I did not have to go through so much that time around.

This new house was two-story with six bedrooms and three full bathrooms. It was fully loaded! Long story short, we moved into a new house. God then spoke and told me He was not in the decision. After we settled into the house, I heard God say, "You did it anyway?" I knew that wasn't good, but I was so consumed with my desire for bigger and better that I ignored that small still voice. God let me know I was disobedient, and we needed to go back to the first home we signed the papers to get. I asked for instructions because I had no clue how. I then received a call from the company's representative that dealt with the first home we signed the papers to lease in order to buy.

He told me my realtor was not honest with me and only after personal gain. He pleaded with me to go back to the first home, and after six months, things would be financially better. I told him I could not go back. All I could think about was the joy on our children's faces once they found out they were getting their own room. How was I going to break the news to the kids? I knew that would be upsetting for them. So, I decided to stay in the second house. I was disobeying God and pushing away the company's representative that was only trying to help me. The representative called me one last time and told me I was making a big mistake and would regret my decision to stay in the second house.

One day trouble hit our house. My husband became very sick and needed surgery immediately! I could not understand what happened because he was doing fine that day. After a couple of months, I was getting hit left and right with bad news. I think the final straw was when we had to move out of our house into a small apartment. We could no longer afford the house, but I knew the root cause of it all was my disobedience to God. He snatched everything away and put me in a "time-out-place" to think about what I had done. The Lord then revealed to me that the first home would have been our investment property after two years of living there. Then we would have had the opportunity to move to another home. God put me on punishment in that small apartment to think about the mistake I had made and to show me He means business.

All I could do was cry because I knew it was my fault. Even then, I still did not learn my lesson. Therefore, the Lord moved us to an even smaller place! That's' when I realized I've got to get this right by following God's guidance. Only then will great things happen. When I started obeying God again, we were blessed with new vehicles and another home. It was not precisely the one I preferred, but I knew God was testing me again. I could not go through those same consequences for a second time. I learned the hard way. It pays to listen to that still small voice. As my mother used to say, "bought sense is the best sense you will have." Disobedience cost us a fortune.

I thought about the scripture *Romans 11:30 NIV*, *"For just as you once were disobedient to God, but now have been shown mercy because of their disobedience."* God still loves and cares for you even when you are disobedient to Him.

5 Ways to let go and Be Free

1. Choose to Be Free daily.

Philippians 4:6-7 NIV, "Do not be anxious about anything, but in every situation, by prayer and petition, with thanksgiving, present your requests to God. And the peace of God, which transcends all understanding, will guard your hearts and your minds in Christ Jesus."
-   We must pray.

- Confess our needs to God. Confess all sin that you've been holding, even the difficult stuff.
- Ask God for help.

He will show you things you were unaware of that have caused your downward spiral into sin or despair. He will lead you to make better decisions. God will lead you to let go of toxic attitudes or relationships, and He will guide you into a healthy new place in Him.

The truth is:

A) Stay at the feet of Jesus

B) Ask God for help

C) Seek to hear His voice

D) Open His word

E) Pray and thank Him for the work He's doing in your life.

That is how we set our minds on the things above. "Fess up when you Mess up!" We cannot operate in our flesh at the same time we try to live out His word. It just doesn't work. We must choose which side we are on.

2) <u>Understand that life is bigger than you.</u>

Proverbs 3:5-6 NIV, "Trust in the Lord with all your heart and lean not on your own understanding; in all your ways submit to him, and he will make your paths straight."

Sometimes, we will know the right things to do yet struggle to do it. We fall short when we don't do the right thing. Oftentimes, it's a battle to trust that God's ways are better.

We might think He messed up, forgot us, He doesn't really care about us, or understand how complex this world might be. We start to believe that we know better somehow when God is all-knowing because He created everything. I tend to battle with this on occasions. God does not need our help with doing anything or knowing what is best. We sometimes hurry along and do not stop to see if we are headed in the right direction. God should always be directing our path. God never asked us to figure it all out on our own or live in our strength. We need Him to survive.

3) Choose to listen to God's voice and not the lies of the enemy.

John 8:32 NIV, "Then you will know the truth, and the truth will set you free."

God has a plan for our lives, and so does Satan. We must decide which voice we're going to listen to and follow. Chances are, if we don't make a determined choice to follow God, we will fall into the trap of the enemy.

The Bible has several scriptures about the devious schemes of Satan and how he operates:

A) He is a twister of truth

B) He is deceptive

C) The father of lies

John 10:10 NIV, "The thief comes only to steal and kill and destroy; I have come that they may have life, and have it to the full."

Satan knows our weaknesses and will use them to bring us down. God never told us to walk in fear. He does advise us to be watchful and on guard. As we continually press into a relationship with God and meditate on His Word, we will be able to detect deception. God is alive, truth, and the Word.

4) Put on the whole Armor of God.

Ephesians 6:13-18 NIV, "Therefore put on the full armor of God, so that when the day of evil comes, you may be able to stand your ground, and after you have done everything, to stand. Stand firm then, with the belt of truth buckled around your waist, with the breastplate of righteousness in place, and with your feet fitted with the readiness that comes from the gospel of peace. In addition to all this, take up the shield of faith, with which you can extinguish all the flaming arrows of the evil one. Take the helmet of salvation and the sword of the Spirit, which is the word of God. And pray in the Spirit on all occasions with all kinds of prayers and requests. With this in mind, be alert and always keep on praying for all the Lord's people."

God gives specific instructions in His word. He gives us what we need to stand strong in this life so we can keep our eyes on Him. Yet all too often, we are distracted, unprepared, or simply too busy to realize what we're up against or who is the real enemy. The forces of darkness don't wait for us to be ready for its attacks.

The battle is real!

5) Guard your heart, lay aside the old nature, and let go of fear, worry, and sin.

Proverbs 4:23 NIV, "Above all else, guard your heart, for everything you do flows from it."

Those inner thoughts, words, and even what we accept in our lives matter. It holds the power to make or break us. That is more reason to make sure our thinking is based on truth on what God says.

Guard: Protect; to keep safe, your heart-innermost being, which represents the very core of your thoughts, your mind, your action, and decisions, for everything you do flows from it.

Our lives depend on that choice to guard our hearts and set our minds on the things above. When we fill our minds, thoughts, and hearts with the right things, the wrong things won't have any room to enter. God's Word and truth offer protection. Casting our cares on Him by releasing our problems and burdens helps us guard our hearts. We should remember to seek forgiveness over sin, so we can be forgiven by God when we get stuck in a place. Guarding your heart takes effort on our part. Choosing to give God our struggles also requires trust. We must let go and remember that God is in control. We are not set free to fit in. We've been changed to make a difference!

May God help us to walk wisely and live free. May He remind us daily to set our minds on Him. May He give us the power we need to extend love and light to a world that desperately needs His hope, in Jesus's name, Amen.

God brings the best out of us because He develops perfection in us. Begin to look at life from God's perspective! Seek after what God desires for your life. The number one way to see things from God's perspective is to pray to Him daily. Sometimes we must pray through each day. We should also learn to walk with Him and recognize His power and presence in our lives.

God loves us more than we could ever fully and truly know or understand. He longs to help us, and He is always there. God's Word reminds us that He is our strong tower and protection. God promises to draw near to those who seek Him. God is faithful with helping us through the struggles of this world.

Mind of the Spirit

There are things you can do to improve your mind:

- Learn a new word weekly

- Do a puzzle daily

- Read a book (Bible)

- Exercise

- Meditate

- Get plenty of sleep

- Healthy diet

- Remain social

- Change your perspective to match up with the Word of God

Romans 8:5-6 NIV, "Those who live according to the flesh have their minds set on what the flesh desires; but those who live in accordance with the Spirit have their minds set on what the Spirit desires. The mind governed by the flesh is death, but the mind governed by the Spirit is life and peace."

JOURNAL YOUR EXPERIENCE

Philippians 4:7 NIV,
"And the peace of God, which transcends all understanding
will guard your hearts and your minds in Christ Jesus."

Romans 12:2 NIV,
"Do not conform to the pattern of this world, but be transformed
by the renewing of your mind. Then you will be able to test and
approve what God's will is—his good, pleasing and perfect will."

2 Timothy 1:7 NIV,
"For the Spirit God gave us does not make us timid
but gives us power, love and self-discipline."

Note:

CHAPTER 5
Battlefield of The Mind

The battlefield or the realm in which spiritual warfare takes place is in the mind of every believer in Christ. We wrestle with our minds against world systems, the flesh or the carnal nature, and the devil (Satan). Our mind encompasses our thoughts and emotions.

All spiritual battles occur in our minds, but the place in our hearts that we give to Christ determines our victory. I have realized that our thoughts and feelings affect God's will and purpose for our lives.

We seek to live by the truth and power of God because it is our assurance of God's promised victory in each situation in our lives. We are aware of the destruction that surrounds our world daily.

1 Peter 1:5 NIV, "who through faith are shielded by God's power until the coming of the salvation that is ready to be revealed in the last time."

We cannot live a half spiritual and half carnal life because you can jeopardize much victory with Christ. Not even 99.5% will do, God wants it all. We cannot be lukewarm and straddling the fence with accepting Him. When God's laws are followed, we build a sure foundation in Him.

A few examples of being lukewarm for God:

1. Only calling on God when there is a problem.

2. Having the idea that Christianity is "what can God do for me? How can He make my life better?"

3. Disobeying the Word of God and even twisting scripture to justify sin.

4. Living two different lives as hypocrites. Live against God's Word six days a week, then born again Christians that are holy on the seventh day.

5. Compromising morals and values to fit in with the world's views because it's popular.

6. Only wanting to be a Christian to escape hell. Hell is real!

7. No true repentance life and do not want to change.

8. Comparing one's salvation to another.

9. Not having faith in God.

10. Jesus is not one's first desire.

My faith has been tested time and time again. At times, I would think I'm strong enough to fight on my own, but always seem to slip back into my old ways. I would fulfill my own desires and be left off worse than what I started. My thoughts were if I was not doing harm to myself then it was okay to indulge in my desires. Not true! Looking back over my life, I realized I was indeed harming myself because I was going against God's commands. I was not fulfilling my purpose either. It is very dangerous to know your assignment in life and not walk in it. I was distracted by temptation, and I liked it.

In 2019 the Lord told me He was done with my off/on relationship with Him. He consistently wanted all of me. I must be steadfast, unmovable, and always abounding in the works of the Lord. I began to understand what was happening and that I needed to get into my rightful place in God.

1 Peter 5:8 NIV, "Be alert and of sober mind. Your enemy the devil prowls around like a roaring lion looking for someone to devour."

JOURNAL YOUR EXPERIENCE

Philippians 4:7 NIV,
"And the peace of God, which transcends all understanding
will guard your hearts and your minds in Christ Jesus."

Romans 12:2 NIV,
"Do not conform to the pattern of this world, but be transformed
by the renewing of your mind. Then you will be able to test and
approve what God's will is—his good, pleasing and perfect will."

Isaiah 26:3 NIV,
"You will keep in perfect peace those whose minds are steadfast, because they trust in you."

2 Timothy 1:7 NIV,
"For the Spirit God gave us does not make us timid
but gives us power, love and self-discipline."

Note:

CHAPTER 6
New Mindset

Our mindset sets the stage for our lives. We must always be open-minded to receive from God. Open-minded people are destined to grow. A new mindset allows us to be filled with limitless potential and possibilities to know that the sky is the limit. We could dream big and reach beyond the stars. God reminded me to take off the limitations I placed on my life because He is with me, and He is endless. He guides and teaches me through every assignment. If you changed your perspective, you could change your life. Get involved with what God says about your life and leave the rest behind. Allow God to change your life from where it is to be to where it needs to be. Focus on God. He won't lead you astray.

List of mindsets:

Fixed Mindset-

Believe that one's basic qualities, like intelligence or talent, are fixed traits. This mindset remains the same over time with no increase in development. Most people with a fixed mindset oftentimes face failures because they lack growth. These are people who have not realized the TAG- (Talents, Abilities, and Gifts) God has placed on the inside of them.

- Seek God and allow Him to show you who He created you to be. Know that nothing is missing, broken, or lacking in your life. You are perfectly made.

Growth Mindset-

People with this mindset can learn anything or acquire any ability if they put in enough effort. They thrive in challenges and do not describe themselves as a failure. They do not allow setbacks to stop them. They use them as a comeback. A "growth mindset" helps one to be leveled headed, always think ahead, and confidently take risks. People with a "growth mindset" tend to have a healthier perspective on life, be more motivated and more successful. They are visionaries because they know everything will work in their favor.

- I took a risk writing this book because I thought I was not worthy of becoming an author. Since I am willing to develop continually, I knew what God had for me was, in fact, for me. I trust in God. Therefore, everything will work in my favor.

Traditional Mindset-

This mindset is based on systems set in place over a long period of time, such as cultural norms, religion, or family upbringing. Traditional mindset varies from person to person.

- One day I realized I had to change my ways because they did not always line up with the Will of God for my life. I was raised a certain way and even went to a few churches that operated differently. I had to allow God to show me things to omit out of my life and what to carry on. Not everything we are taught is right according to God's desires. Just because it is a good thing does not mean it's the right thing. I had to leave that place of doing things the way I had always done them because the Lord had anointed and appointed me for a purpose bigger than my eyes could see.

We have the power to change our lives. It all starts with our minds. A changed mindset is a step in the right direction for new adventures. I urge you to practice a growth mindset until it becomes a habit. Everything we know had to be taught to us. Why not learn to train your brain to line up with the Word of God?

How To Develop a New Mindset

Change your self-talk-

The conversation you have with yourself is a direct reflection of your mindset.

What are you saying about yourself?

What do you think of yourself?

If you tell yourself you are not good enough to achieve your dreams, it will not happen. Say what you want to see until you see what you said! Change all the negative self-talk to words of affirmation and speak the scriptures of God's Word over your life.

Change your language-

Change the way you tell your story about yourself to others. Change how you speak about your situations.

Avoid phrases like, "I will always end up like this..." "I will always be here..." Make a habit of talking about what is going well in your life instead of what is not. That will give you a mindset of abundance instead of fear and lack. Determine the mindset you need and act as if it has already worked in your favor. Pick a goal to achieve and stick to it. Always have a positive attitude about how the outcome will be.

Look up to others that have achieved the goal you have in place and think of their mindset. Try reaching out to them for guidance on accomplishing your goal. For example, healthy & fit people might share the mentality of valuing their bodies. Therefore, they take care of their bodies by eating healthy meals and exercising daily. If this is your goal, begin to act as if you are already there. This change in mindset would trick your brain into adopting the change in your life as you reinforce your new perspective with action. Don't just talk about it; be about it.

Learn & apply-

Don't just gather information. Take it and put it to use. You will begin to see results that way. Refresh and renew your mind daily. Read books about how the mind and brain work. Learn from the experts through in-person or online courses.

Surround yourself with people who match your mindset if you want to upgrade things in your life. Sit with people who are successful in what they do. It is easier to adopt a new outlook when it is already working for other people. Learn how they think and adapt their daily habits to match their mindset. (POSITIVE VIBES ONLY)

I remember when my family and I relocated to Texas. We did not know many people, but my husband formed a bond with a client we gained and even learned from him. The client was prospering in all his businesses and showed my husband how he did it. The client even introduced my husband to friends so he could establish a relationship and later gain them as a client as well. The client knew somebody who knew somebody that passed along the word concerning our services. Then our business grew from there. If you are familiar with Southlake, Texas, you would know that it is a prosperous area filled with top-named wealthy people. That is also the area my husband received most projects as a result of taking advice from that one client who introduced him to others. Connections are important. God moved for my husband so that he could flourish in his God-given skillset!!

What a mighty God we serve! God will connect you to the right people if you remain obedient to Him! Don't be afraid to reach out and talk to people. The very one you may not want to get to know maybe attach to your next blessing! Begin working on your new mindset today because God has so much in store for each of you!

A New Mindset Taught Me:

- To not sit in places where others did not respect me.

- To allow God to move me as He chose.

- To carefully answer questions.

- To think outside the box. God told me to move the box so I did not trip and fall back in.

- To not accept every invitation extended to me.

- To stop trying to save the world.

- To be the best wife, mother, and grandmother I could be.

- To understand "labor of love" is over!

- To shift from "I don't know if I can" to "I will do it to the best of my ability."

- To stop feeling sorry for those who do not take care of their responsibilities and priorities.

- To understand "help" is not just in the form of money, but Godly advice. It works!!!

- To not give to the greedy, but the needy.

- To pay close attention to the word "love" because it is an action word. It isn't just something to say. Love is what love does! What are you doing? Is it love?

- To walk in confidence through the doors the Lord has opened for me.

- To encourage others even when my world is turned upside down.

- To understand that actions speak louder than words. God reminded me that people would say anything and do something different.

- To keep my moves private and move in complete silence.

- To release what God tells me at the opportune time.

- To not trust everyone and pay close attention to their motive for wanting to be a part of my life.

- To not speak prematurely.

- To live my life totally in this order: God, husband, children, grandchildren, and everything else rightfully connected to me.

- To know the category to place people in my life.

- To watch as well as pray.

- To leave those behind who are always in competition with me.

- To leave all the small talk behind and think bigger.

- To not think everyone will support and be happy for me.

- To keep my mouth closed and my eyes and ears open wide because God is speaking!

- To remain on fire for God.

- To never go back to life without God.

- To believe what people do instead of what they say.

- To keep my eyes on the prize which is my Father in heaven!

- To pray before answering a question because it is critical for obedience.

- To hear and obey my Father in heaven.

- To not go to others when God gives me a specific assignment.
- To connect with winning women.
- To leave anger behind me. God has me in the palm of His hand!
- To live in a place of complete peace!
- To accept deliverance from God when there is a need.
- To accept healing from God when there is a need.
- To accept that I am enough in the sight of my Heavenly Father and to do His will!

I could go on and on, but you get my drift!

JOURNAL YOUR EXPERIENCE

Philippians 4:7 NIV,
"And the peace of God, which transcends all understanding,
will guard your hearts and your minds in Christ Jesus."

Romans 12:2 NIV,
"Do not conform to the pattern of this world, but be transformed
by the renewing of your mind. Then you will be able to test and
approve what God's will is—his good, pleasing and perfect will."

Isaiah 26:3 NIV,
"You will keep in perfect peace those whose minds are steadfast, because they trust in you."

2 Timothy 1:7 NIV,
"For the Spirit God gave us does not make us timid
but gives us power, love and self-discipline."

Note:

CHAPTER 7
Freedom in The Mind

Do not allow Satan to live rent-free in your head. Know that the devil's playground refers to our mind. That is where the temptation or influence starts. Satan will plant evil or sinful activity in our minds with hopes that we carry it out.

James 4:7 NIV, "Submit yourselves, then, to God. Resist the devil, and he will flee from you."

1 Peter 5:7 KJV, "Casting all your care upon him; for he careth for you."

Do not give Satan any footholds or entryways of sin to gain access into your mind. For example, if someone hurts or offends you, do not hold a grudge. Forgive them quickly and move forward. Forgiveness is for you and not the other person. Forgive so that God can forgive you and you're able to be at peace.

Matthew 6:14-15 NIV, "For if you forgive other people when they sin against you, your heavenly Father will also forgive you. But if you do not forgive others their sins, your Father will not forgive your sins."

When we forgive one another, Satan has no door to enter because sin is the key that unlocks the door. Unforgiveness is sin. Do not fall into the temptation of any sin. If Satan can control your mind, he will use you like a puppet on a string under his control. Our minds lead our words and actions.

Stay rooted and grounded in the Word of God. Remember, Satan loves to target the vulnerable, broken-hearted, feebleminded, naïve, those who are easy to be persuaded, and followers. Stay alert! We must keep our minds focused and fixated on God. He will cover, keep, and protect us. Satan is no match for God. Therefore, stay hidden in God's shadow by obeying and following Him.

Philippians 3:13 KJV, "Brethren, I count not myself to have apprehended: but this one thing I do, forgetting those things which are behind, and reaching forth unto those things which are before,"

Repent of all your sins, ask God for forgiveness, and do not look back!

Freestanding

Stand on God's Word, trusting Him in everything. Do not place your trust in people, including your family and spouse. Do not even extend your trust to your job or resources, but in God alone.

Daniel 10:19 NIV, "Do not be afraid, you who are highly esteemed," he said. "Peace! Be strong now; be strong." When he spoke to me, I was strengthened and said, "Speak, my Lord, since you have given me strength."

It is impossible to stand without the help of God. What is impossible with man is possible with God. The angel of the Lord appeared to Daniel to reveal his future and to strengthen him. The angel of the Lord gave Daniel words of encouragement. Look for God everywhere and in everything that you do. If you can not find God in it, put Him there. He is truly our strength!

Learn to stand with God. He is on your side. Let all burdens, insecurities, and negative thoughts go and give them to God. He can handle it better than we can!

When I was a child, my parents assisted me with learning to walk. After so many falls, they figured that if I fell enough, I would be motivated enough to walk on my own. Looking back, I realize I needed help with keeping my balance, and I would have never learned to walk if it was not for God holding me up. God is the same yesterday, today, and forever. Therefore, He could perform that same miracle today!

God reminded me that a "just man" falls seven times, but he can rise again. It's not too late for you to move forward. Get back up again and keep striving ahead.

Galatians 5:1 KJV, "Stand fast therefore in the liberty wherewith Christ hath made us free, and be not entangled again with the yoke of bondage."

God has broken the yoke of bondage and slavery. Know that you are free and can stand on your own two feet. Hold your balance. Help is available and on the way because God is with you always. God is on our side and wants you to prosper. You cannot look to others for what

God alone can give. He is my all and all. Are you going to allow Him to become yours?

John 14:27 NIV, "Peace I leave with you; my peace I give you. I do not give to you as the world gives. Do not let your hearts be troubled and do not be afraid."

God has you and me in the palm of His hand. Believe that you can receive from the Lord.

Free from making excuses

Excuse-

Attempt to lessen the blame attaching to (a fault or offense) seek to defend or justify. Release (someone) from a duty or requirement from a responsibility.

A few common excuses:

During prayer
- I don't know how to pray.

- I prayed, and nothing happened.

- I can't pray like you.

While reading and studying the Bible
- I do not understand.

- I've been busy.

- I cannot stay focused.

When blaming others instead of taking responsibility
- I would not have done that if...

- They should not have said...

- I'm only like this when...

- Normally I act better than this if...

For missing church
- I don't understand what the Pastor is teaching.

- I can't follow their principles.

- I haven't found a church I would like to attend.

For not exercising

- I will start at the beginning of the year.

- I'm just not motivated to do it.

- I don't have an accountability partner to help me stay focused.

- My partner likes me the way I am.

- It's too hot/cold outside.

- The gym is temporarily closed.

For eating unhealthy

- I know this is not good for me, but it sure does taste good.

- I only cook this because I got off work late.

- I'll start eating better next week.

- I can't help myself.

- My parents are great cooks, and I just can't say no.

- Healthy food is too expensive.

The ultimate blame game

Genesis 3:11-13 NIV, "And he said, "Who told you that you were naked? Have you eaten from the tree that I commanded you not to eat from?" The man said, "The woman you put here with me—she gave me some fruit from the tree, and I ate it." Then the Lord God said to the woman, "What is this you have done?" The woman said, "The serpent deceived me, and I ate."

Adam and Eve were fully aware that they could not eat from the Tree of Knowledge in the center of the garden but decided to do it anyway. They got caught by God and blamed someone else instead of owning up to their actions. Adam blamed Eve and Eve blamed the serpent (Satan), who deceived them both.

Did you locate yourself in an excuse category? I am sure you answered, "yes." I understand because I was once there, but now is the time to get it right. Time does not wait for anyone.

Matthew 12:36 NIV, "But I tell you that everyone will have to give account on the day of judgment for every empty word they have spoken."

Time out for excuses! If you make up one excuse, you will have many others that will follow. There is a thin line between excuses and lies. Be careful!

Don't allow excuses to keep you from living the best life God has for you. Be stronger and better than those excuses. An excuse is never going to be anything other than an excuse. Think about it.

Excuses never...
- Graduate to the next level

- Pay a bill

- Held a job or career

- Acquired health or wealth

- Been anything other than an excuse
John 8:36 NIV, "So if the Son sets you free, you will be free indeed."

Let's break the chains of sin and excuses that have held us back from our divine inheritance. Live in Freedom Now!

THE LORD'S PRAYER

"After this manner therefore pray ye: Our Father which art in heaven, Hallowed be thy name. Thy kingdom come. Thy will be done in earth, as it is in heaven. Give us this day our daily bread. And forgive us our debts, as we forgive our debtors. And lead us not into temptation, but deliver us from evil: For thine is the kingdom, and the power, and the glory, forever. Amen.

JOURNAL YOUR EXPERIENCE

Philippians 4:7 NIV,
"And the peace of God, which transcends all understanding
will guard your hearts and your minds in Christ Jesus."

Romans 12:2 NIV,
"Do not conform to the pattern of this world, but be transformed
by the renewing of your mind. Then you will be able to test and
approve what God's will is—his good, pleasing and perfect will."

Isaiah 26:3 NIV,
"You will keep in perfect peace those whose minds are
steadfast, because they trust in you."

2 Timothy 1:7 NIV,
"For the Spirit God gave us does not make us timid,
but gives us power, love and self-discipline."

Note:

Notes:

What did you learn from my life?

_____

_____

_____

_____

_____

_____

_____

_____

How can you apply what you learned to your life?

_____

_____

_____

_____

_____

_____

_____

_____

If you were in my shoes, what would you do different?

_____

_____

_____

_____

_____

_____

_____

_____